Elgar Organ Album

Book 2

NOVELLO PUBLISHING LIMITED
8/9 Frith Street, London W1V 5TZ

Order No: NOV 010995

CONTENTS

NIMROD
from 'Enigma Variations'
Opus 36

Arranged by W. H. HARRIS

*Only if the Solo Tuba is enclosed and an effective crescendo possible

TRIUMPHAL MARCH
from 'Caractacus'
Opus 35

IV Solo (Reeds 8')
III Swell
II Great
I Choir

Arranged by
EDWIN H. LEMARE

30330

più animato

8

12

allargando al Tempo I

cantabile e largamente

FUNERAL MARCH
from 'Grania and Diarmid'
Opus 42

Arranged by
BASIL RAMSEY

Maestoso ♩ = 66

20

PRELUDE AND ANGEL'S FAREWELL
from 'The Dream of Gerontius'
Opus 38

Arranged by
A. HERBERT BREWER

26

20230

28

29

32

20230

ANGEL'S FAREWELL

Andante tranquillo ♪ = 92
Sw. Open Diapason

38